baby cashmerino 3

contents

introduction

baby cashmerino 3 is the latest addition to my popular series of booklets for babies and children, all knitted in one of my favourite yarns. This collection features a range of designs from a smart cabled slipover and pretty dress for special occasions, playful alphabet cubes for the nursery, and for the newly born there is a delicate lace and bobble blanket to be wrapped and cherished in.

baby cashmerino is the perfect yarn for babies, soft against the skin, easy to wash and wear and for those of us who love to knit for the little ones in our lives, a joy to knit with.

Debbie Bliss

basic information

The quantities of yarn are based on average requirements and are therefore approximate. It is essential to work to the stated tension and you should always knit a tension square before starting. If you have too many stitches to 10cm/4in your tension is tight and you should change to a larger needle. If there are too few stitches, your tension is loose and you should change to a smaller needle. We cannot accept responsibility for the finished product if any yarn other than the one specified is used. Instructions given are for the first size, with larger sizes in round brackets. Where only one figure or instruction is given this applies to all sizes.

Work all directions inside square brackets the number of times stated. See ball band for washing and pressing instructions.

standard abbreviations

alt = alternate
beg = beginning
cont = continue
dec = decrease
foll = following
inc = increase
k = knit
kfb = knit into front and back of st
m1 = make one st by picking up the loop lying between st just worked and next st and working into back of it
p = purl
pfb = purl into front and back of st
patt = pattern
psso = pass slipped st over
rem = remaining
rep = repeat
skpo = slip 1, knit 1, pass slipped stitch over
sl = slip
ssk = [sl 1 knitwise] twice, insert tip of left needle from left to right through front of both sts and k2tog
st(s) = stitch(es)
st st = stocking stitch
tbl = through back loop
tog = together
yf = yarn forward
yo = yarn over needle
yrn = yarn round needle

USA glossary

cast off = bind off
moss stitch = seed stitch
tension = gauge
stocking stitch = stockinette stitch
yarn forward, yarn over needle, or yarn round needle = yarn over

smock coat

beret and socks

blanket

teddy rattle

alphabet cubes

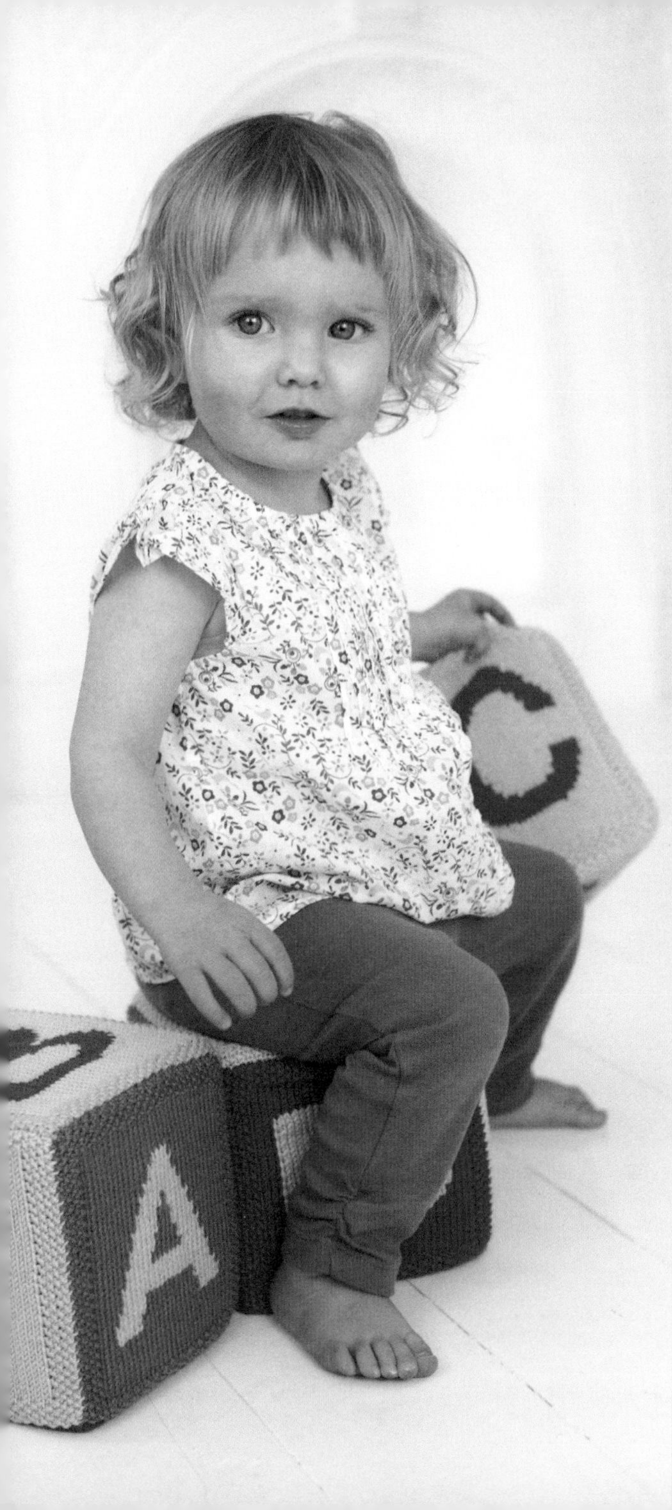

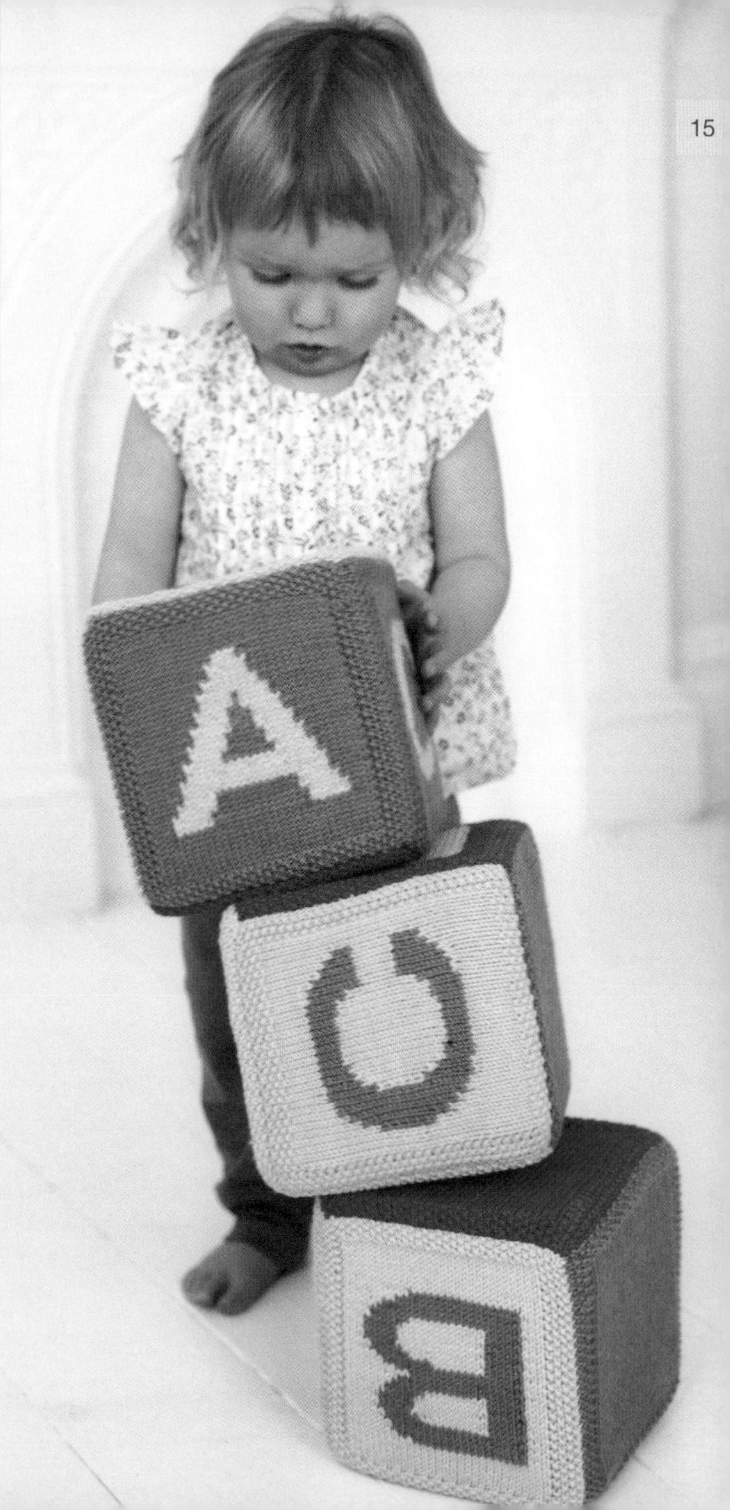

bear faced pyjama case

cable tank top

lucy locket dress

star sweater

smock coat

measurements

to fit ages (months)

3–6   6–12   12–18   18–24

finished measurements

chest

54	60	67	74	cm
21¼	23½	26½	29¼	in

length

36	39	43	50	cm
14¼	15½	17	19¾	in

sleeve length

16	18	20	23	cm
6¼	7	8	9	in

materials

- 5(6:7:7) 50g balls Debbie Bliss baby cashmerino in Linen 005.
- Pair each 3mm (US 2–3) and 3¼mm (US 3) knitting needles.
- 3(3:4:4) buttons.

tension

25 sts and 34 rows to 10cm/4in square over st st using 3¼mm (US 3) needles.

abbreviations

See page 7.

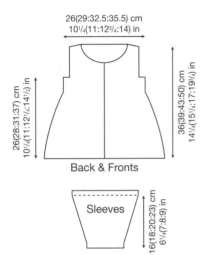

26(29:32.5:35.5) cm
10¼(11:12¾:14) in

26(28:31:37) cm
10¼(11:12¼:14½) in

36(39:43:50) cm
14¼(15¼:17:19¾) in

Back & Fronts

Sleeves

16(18:20:23) cm
6¼(7:8:9) in

back

With 3mm (US 2-3) needles,
cast on 97(109:121:133) sts.
Next row K1, [p1, k1] to end.
This row **forms** the moss st.
Work 5 more rows.
Change to 3¼mm (US 3) needles.
Beg with a k row, work in st st
until back measures
21(23:26:32)cm/8¼(9:10¼:12½)in
from cast on edge, ending with
a k row.
Dec row (wrong side) P1, [p2tog,
p1] to end. 65(73:81:89)sts.
Change to 3mm (US 2-3) needles
and work in patt as follows:
1st row K4, [p1, k7] to last 5 sts,
p1, k4.
2nd row P3, [k1, p1, k1, p5] to
last 6 sts, k1, p1, k1, p3.

3rd row K2, [p1, k3] to last 3 sts,
p1, k2.
4th row P1, [k1, p5, k1, p1] to end.
5th row P1, [k7, p1] to end.
6th row As 4th row.
7th row As 3rd row.
8th row As 2nd row.
These 8 rows **form** the patt and
are repeated throughout.
Cont in patt until back measures
26(28:31:37)cm/10¼(11:12¼:14½)in
from cast on edge, ending with a
wrong side row.
Shape armholes
Cast off 8 sts at beg of next 2 rows.
49(57:65:73) sts.
Cont straight until back measures
36(39:43:50)cm/14¼(15¼:17:19¾)in
from cast on edge, ending with a
wrong side row.
Shape shoulders
Cast off 7(8:10:11) sts at beg of
next 2 rows and 7(9:10:12) sts at
beg of foll 2 rows.
Cast off rem 21(23:25:27) sts.

left front

With 3mm (US 2-3) needles,
cast on 48(54:60:66) sts.
1st row [P1, k1] to end.
2nd row [K1, p1] to end.
These 2 rows **form** the moss st.
Work 4 more rows.
Change to 3¼mm (US 3) needles.
Next row (right side) K to last
5 sts, moss st 5.

Next row Moss st 5, p to end.
These 2 rows **form** st st with
moss st front border.
Cont in patt until front measures
21(23:26:32)cm/8¼(9:10¼:12½)in
from cast on edge, ending with
a right side row.
Dec row (wrong side) Moss st 5,
[p1, p2tog] 14(16:18:20) times, p1.
34(38:42:46) sts.
Change to 3mm (US 2-3) needles
and work in patt as follows:
1st and 3rd sizes only
1st row K4, [p1, k7] to last 6 sts,
p1, moss st 5.
2nd row Moss st 5, p1, k1, p5,
[k1, p1, k1, p5] to last 6 sts, k1,
p1, k1, p3.
3rd row K2, [p1, k3] to last 8 sts,
p1, k2, moss st 5.
4th row Moss st 5, p3, k1, p1,
[k1, p5, k1, p1] to end.
5th row P1, [k7, p1] to last 9 sts,
k4, moss st 5.
6th row As 4th row.
7th row As 3rd row.
8th row As 2nd row.
2nd and 4th sizes only
1st row K4, [p1, k7] to last 10 sts,
p1, k4, moss st 5.
2nd row Moss st 5, p3, [k1, p1,
k1, p5] to last 6 sts, k1, p1, k1, p3.
3rd row K2, [p1, k3] to last 8 sts,
p1, k2, moss st 5.
4th row Moss st 5, p1, [k1, p5,
k1, p1] to end.

5th row P1, [k7, p1] to last 5 sts, moss st 5.
6th row As 4th row.
7th row As 3rd row.
8th row As 2nd row.

All sizes
These 8 rows **form** the patt and are repeated throughout.
Cont in patt until front measures 26(28:31:37)cm/10¼(11:12¼:14½)in from cast on edge, ending with a wrong side row.

Shape armhole
Cast off 8 sts at beg of next row. 26(30:34:38) sts.
Cont straight until front measures 32(34:38:45)cm/12½(13½:15:17¾)in from cast on edge, ending with a right side row.

Shape neck
Next row Cast off 3 sts, patt to end.
Next row Patt to last 2 sts, leave these 2 sts on a safety pin.
Dec one st at neck edge on every row until 14(17:20:23) sts rem.
Cont straight until front measures same as Back to shoulder, ending at side edge.

Shape shoulder
Cast off 7(8:10:11) sts at beg of next row.
Work 1 row.
Cast off rem 7(9:10:12) sts .
Mark positions for buttons, the first level with first row of yoke, the 3rd(3rd:4th:4th) 1cm/½in below neck shaping with the remaining 1(1:2:2) spaced evenly between.

right front

Buttonhole row (right side) K1, p1, yo, p2tog, k1, patt to end.
With 3mm (US 2-3) needles, cast on 48(54:60:66) sts.
1st row [K1, p1] to end.
2nd row [P1, k1] to end.
These 2 rows **form** the moss st.
Work 4 more rows.
Change to 3¼mm (US 3) needles.
Next row (right side) Moss st 5, k to end.
Next row P to last 5 sts, moss st 5.
These 2 rows **set** the position of the st st with moss st front border.
Cont in patt until front measures 21(23:26:32)cm/8¼(9:10¼:12½)in from cast on edge, ending with a right side row.
Dec row P1, [p2tog, p1] 14(16:18:20) times, moss st 5. 34(38:42:46) sts.
Change to 3mm (US 2-3) needles and work in patt as follows:

1st and 3rd sizes only
1st row Moss st 5, [p1, k7] to last 5 sts, p1, k4.
2nd row, P3, [k1, p1, k1, p5] to last 7 sts, k1, p1, moss st 5.
3rd row Moss st 5, k2, [p1, k3] to last 3 sts, p1, k2.
4th row, P1, [k1, p5, k1, p1] to last 9 sts, k1, p3, moss st 5.
5th row Moss st 5, k4, p1, [k7, p1] to end.
6th row As 4th row.
7th row As 3rd row.
8th row As 2nd row.

2nd and 4th sizes only
1st row Moss st 5, k4, [p1, k7] to last 5 sts, p1, k4.
2nd row P3, [k1, p1, k1, p5] to last 11 sts, k1, p1, k1, p3, moss st 5.
3rd row Moss st 5, k2, [p1, k3] to last 3 sts, p1, k2.
4th row, P1, [k1, p5, k1, p1] to last 5 sts, moss st 5.
5th row Moss st 5, p1, [k7, p1] to end.
6th row As 4th row.
7th row As 3rd row.
8th row As 2nd row.

All sizes
These 8 rows **form** the patt and are repeated throughout.
Cont in patt until front measures 26(28:31:37)cm/10¼(11:12¼:14½)in from cast on edge, ending with a right side row.

Shape armhole
Cast off 8 sts at beg of next row. 26(30:34:38) sts.
Cont straight until front measures 32(34:38:45)cm/12½(13½:15:17¾)in from cast on edge, ending with a wrong side row.

Shape neck
Next row Cast off 3 sts, moss st next st, leave these 2 sts on a safety pin, patt to end.
Dec one st at neck edge on every row until 14(17:20:23) sts rem.
Cont straight until front measures same as Back to shoulder, ending at side edge.

Shape shoulder

Cast off 7(8:10:11) sts at beg of next row.
Work 1 row.
Cast off rem 7(9:10:12) sts .

sleeves

With 3mm (US 2-3) needles, cast on 31(33:37:39) sts.
Moss st row P1, [k1, p1] to end.
This row **forms** the moss st.
Work 4 more rows.
Inc row (wrong side) Moss st 3(4:6:7), [m1, moss st 5] 5 times, m1, moss st 3(4:6:7). 37(39:43:45) sts.
Change to 3¼ mm (US 3) needles.
Beg with a k row, work in st st.
Work 2 rows.
Inc row (right side) K3, m1, k to last 3 sts, m1, k3.
Work 3 rows.
Rep the last 4 rows 5(7:9:12) times more and the inc row again.
51(57:65:73) sts.
Cont straight until sleeve measures 11(13:15:18)cm/4¼(5:6:7)in from cast on edge, ending with a wrong side row.
1st row K13(16:16:20), [p1, k7] 3(3:4:4) times, p1, k13(16:16:20).
2nd row P12(15:15:19), [k1, p1, k1, p5] 3(3:4:4) times, k1, p1, k1, p12(15:15:19).
3rd row K11(14:14:18), [p1, k3] 7(7:9:9) times, p1, k11(14:14:18).
4th row P10(13:13:17), [k1, p5, k1, p1] 4(4:5:5) times, p9(12:12:16).

5th row K9(12:12:16), p1, [k7, p1] 4(4:5:5) times, k9(12:12:16).
6th row As 4th row.
7th row As 3rd row.
8th row As 2nd row.
Rep 1st to 8th rows twice more then 1st row again.
Cast off.

collar

Join shoulder seams.
With right side facing and 3¼ mm (US 3) needles, slip 2 sts from right front pin onto a needle, pick up and k15(16:17:17) sts up right front neck to shoulder, 31(33:35:37) sts evenly across back neck cast off edge, 15(16:17:17) sts down left front neck, then moss st 2 sts on left front pin. 65(69:73:75)sts.
Next row Moss st 4, k to last 4 sts, moss st 4.
This row **forms** st st with 4 sts in moss st at each end.
Next 2 rows Patt to last 15 sts, turn.
Next 2 rows Patt to last 12 sts, turn.
Next 2 rows Patt to last 9 sts, turn.
Next 2 rows Patt to last 6 sts, turn.
Next row Patt to end.
Work a further 16 rows.
Work 4 rows in moss st.
Cast of in moss st.

pockets (make 2)

With 3mm (US 2-3) needles, cast on 23 sts.
Next row K1, [p1, k1] to end.
This row **forms** the moss st.
Work 3 more rows.
1st row Moss st 3, k4, p1, k7, p1, k4, moss st 3.
2nd row Moss st 3, p3, k1, p1, k1, p5, k1, p1, k1, p3, moss st 3.
3rd row Moss st 3, k2, [p1, k3] 3 times, p1, k2, moss st 3.
4th row Moss st 3, p1, [k1, p5, k1, p1] twice, moss st 3.
5th row Moss st 3, p1, [k7, p1] twice, moss st 3.
6th row As 4th row.
7th row As 3rd row.
8th row As 2nd row.
These 8 rows **form** the patt and are repeated twice more then the 1st row again.
Work 3 rows in moss st.
Cast off in moss st.

to make up

Sew sleeves into armholes with last 9 row ends sewn to sts cast off at underarm. Join side and sleeve seams. Sew on buttons. Sew on pockets.

hooded top

measurements

to fit ages (months)

| 3–6 | 6–9 | 9–12 | 12–18 | 18–24 |

finished measurements

chest

| 51 | 56 | 61 | 65 | 70 | cm |
| 20 | 22 | 24 | 25½ | 27½ | in |

length to shoulder

| 24 | 26 | 28 | 32 | 36 | cm |
| 9½ | 10¼ | 11 | 12½ | 14¼ | in |

sleeve length

| 15 | 17 | 19 | 22 | 24 | cm |
| 6 | 6¾ | 7½ | 8¾ | 9½ | in |

materials

- 4(4:5:5:5) 50g balls of Debbie Bliss baby cashmerino in Pale Green 018.
- Pair each of 3mm (US 2–3) and 3¼ mm (US 3) knitting needles.
- 3¼ mm (US 3) circular needle.
- 3mm (US D/3) crochet hook.

tension

25 sts and 34 rows to 10cm/4in square over st st using 3¼ mm (US 3) needles.

abbreviations

See page 7.

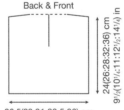

Back & Front

26.5(29:31:33.5:36) cm
10½(11½:12¼:13¼:14¼) in

24(26:28:32:36) cm
9½(10¼:11:12½:14¼) in

Sleeves

15(17:19:22:24) cm
6(6¾:7½:8¾:9½) in

back

With 3mm (US 2-3) needles, cast on 66(72:78:84:90) sts.
K 7 rows.
Change to 3¼ mm (US 3) needles.
Next row (right side) K to end.
Next row K4, p to last 4 sts, k4.
These 2 rows **form** st st with garter st at each end for side vents.
Rep the last 2 rows 4 times more.
Beg with a k row, work in st st until back measures 24(26:28:32:36)cm/9½(10¼:11:12½:14¼)in from cast on edge, ending with a p row.
Shape shoulders
Cast off 9(10:11:12:13) sts at beg of next 4 rows.
Cast off rem 30(32:34:36:38) sts.

front

Work as given for Back until front measures 14(16:18:20:22)cm/5½(6¼:7:8:8¾)in from cast on edge, ending with a p row.
Front opening
Next row K33(36:39:42:45), turn and work on these sts only for left front, leave rem sts on a spare needle.
Next row K4, p to end.
Next row K to end.
Rep the last 2 rows until front measures same as Back to shoulder, ending at side edge.
Shape shoulder
Cast off 9(10:11:12:13) sts at beg of next and foll right side row.
15(16:17:18:19) sts.

Next row K4, p to end.
Leave these sts on a holder.
With right side facing, rejoin yarn
to sts on spare needle, k to end.
Next row P to last 4 sts, k4.
Next row K to end.
Rep the last 2 rows until front
measures the same as Back
to shoulder shaping, ending
at side edge.
Shape shoulder
Cast off 9(10:11:12:13) sts at beg
of next and foll wrong side row.
Leave rem 15(16:17:18:19) sts
on the needle.

hood

Next row (right side)
K15(16:17:18:19) sts from right front,
cast on 45(48:51:54:57) sts, k across
15(16:17:18:19) sts from left front
holder. 75(80:83:90:95) sts.
Next row K4, p to last 4 sts, k4.
Next row K37(39:41:45:47), m1,
k1, m1, k to end.
Work 5 rows in st st with garter st
edges.
Next row K38(40:42:46:48), m1,
k1, m1, k to end.
Cont in this way, increasing 2 sts
in centre of every foll 6th row until
there are 97(104:109:118:125) sts.
Cont straight until hood measures
20(22:24:26:28)cm/8(8¾:9½:10¼:11)in,
ending with a wrong side row.
Cast off.

sleeves

With 3mm (US 2–3) needles,
cast on 34(36:38:40:42) sts.
K 7 rows.
Change to 3¼mm (US 3) needles.
Beg with a k row, work in st st.
Work 2 rows.
Inc row K3, m1, k to last 3 sts,
m1, k3.
Work 3 rows.
Rep the last 4 rows 8(10:12:14:16)
times more and the inc row again.
54(60:66:72:78) sts.
Cont straight until sleeve measures
15(17:19:22:24)cm/6(6¾:7½:8¾:9½)in
from cast on edge, ending with
a p row.
Cast off.

front fastening

With 3¼mm (US 3) needles and yarn
used double, make a slip loop on left
hand needle.
Next row [K1, p1, k1] all into slip
loop, turn, p3, turn, k3, turn, p3,
slip 1, k2tog, psso, pull up and
secure.
With 3mm (US D/3) crochet hook
and yarn used double, make a
3cm/1¼in chain.

to make up

Join shoulder seams. Sew cast on
edge of hood to cast off sts at back
neck, easing to fit. Fold hood in half
and join top seam. With centre of cast
off edge of sleeve to shoulder, sew on
sleeves. Join sleeve seams. Join side
seams to top of garter st opening.
Stitch bobble to right front garter
stitch edge, then make a loop from
the chain and stitch to left front edge
to match.

beret and socks

size

to fit ages (months)
3–6   6–9

materials

beret

- One 50g ball of Debbie Bliss
  baby cashmerino in each of
  Sage Green 019 (A), Peach 022 (B),
  Burnt Orange 023 (C), Pale Green
  018 (D) and Mustard 020 (E).

socks

- One 50g ball of Debbie Bliss
  baby cashmerino in Sage Green 019
  (A) and oddments in each of Peach
  022 (B), Burnt Orange 023 (C), Pale
  Green 018 (D) and Mustard 020 (E).
- Pair each 3mm (US 2–3) and 3¼mm
  (US 3) knitting needles.

tensions

25 sts and 52 rows to 10cm/4in
square over garter st and 25 sts
and 34 rows over st st, both using
3¼mm (US 3) needles.

abbreviations

See page 7.

tip

The beret and socks can be made
from one 50g ball in each of the
contrast colours B, C, D and E, but
each will need one complete ball of A.

beret stripe pattern

5 rows A, 2 rows B, 4 rows C, 2 rows
D, 2 rows E, 4 rows B, 2 rows A,
4 rows D, 2 rows C, 6 rows A, 4 rows
E, 2 rows D, 2 rows B, 4 rows C,
2 rows E, 2 rows A, 2 rows D, 2 rows
C, 4 rows B, 2 rows A, 2 rows B,
2 rows E, 4 rows D, 2 rows C, 4 rows
A, 2 rows E, 4 rows B, 2 rows D and
4 rows C.

beret

With 3¼mm (US 3) needles and A,
cast on 82(98) sts.
K 5 rows.
Inc row K4(6), [m1, k1, m1, k11(13)]
6 times, m1, k1, m1, k5(7). 96(112) sts.
K 5 rows.
Inc row K5(7), [m1, k1, m1, k13(15)]
6 times, m1, k1, m1, k6(8).110(126) sts.
K 5 rows.
Inc row K6(8), [m1, k1, m1, k15(17)]
6 times, m1, k1, m1, k7(9).
124(140) sts.
K 5 rows.
Inc row K7(9), [m1, k1, m1, k17(19)]
6 times, m1, k1, m1, k8(10).
138(154) sts.
K 5(7) rows.
Inc row K8(10), [m1, k1, m1, k19(21)]
6 times, m1, k1, m1, k9(11).
152(168) sts.
K 4 rows.

Dec row K7(9), [skpo, k1, k2tog, k17(19)] 6 times, skpo, k1, k2tog, k8(10). 138(154) sts.
K 4 rows.
Dec row K6(8), [skpo, k1, k2tog, k15(17)] 6 times, skpo, k1, k2tog, k7(9). 124(140) sts.
K 4 rows.
Dec row K5(7), [skpo, k1, k2tog, k13(15)] 6 times, skpo, k1, k2tog, k6(8). 110(126) sts.
K 4 rows.
Cont in this way to dec 14 sts across next and every foll 5th row until 26(28) sts rem.
Next row K2tog 1(0) time, [ssk, k2tog] to end. 13(14) sts.
K 1 row.
1st size only
Next row K1, [k2tog, ssk] to end. 7 sts.
2nd size only
Next row Ssk, [k2tog, ssk] to end. 7 sts.
Break yarn, thread through rem sts, pull up and secure.
Join seam, choosing whether to make up with the definite stripes or the muted stripes as the right side. We made ours with the muted stripes as the right side.

socks (make 2)

With 3¼ mm (US 3) needles and A, cast on 36(40) sts.
K 1 row.
K 2 rows C, 2 rows B, 2 rows D, 2 rows E, 2 rows C, 2 rows D and 2 rows A.
Beg with a p row, work in st st in A only.
Work 1 row.
Dec row K5, k2tog, k to last 7 sts, skpo, k5.
Work 3(5) rows.
Dec row K4, k2tog, k to last 6 sts, skpo, k4.
Work 3(5) rows.
Dec row K3, [k2tog, k6(7)] 3 times, k2tog, k3(4). 28(32) sts.
Work 2(4) rows.
Shape heel
Next row P8(9) sts only, turn.
Work 9 rows in st st on these 8(9) sts only.
Dec row P2(3), p2tog, p1, turn.
Next row Sl 1, k3(4).
Dec row P3(4), p2tog, p1, turn.
Next row Sl 1, k4(5).
Dec row P4(5), p2tog, break yarn.
Leave rem 5(6) sts on a holder.
With wrong side facing, rejoin yarn to rem sts, p next 12(14) sts, slip these sts onto a holder, p to end.
Work 8 rows in st st on these 8(9) sts.
Dec row K2(3), ssk, k1, turn.
Next row Sl 1, p3(4).
Dec row K3(4), ssk, k1, turn.
Next row Sl 1, p4(5).

Dec row K4(5), ssk, turn.
Next row Sl 1, p4(5).
Shape instep
Next row K5(6), pick up and k8 sts evenly along inside edge of heel, k12(14) sts from holder, pick up and k8 sts along inside edge of heel and k5(6) sts from holder. 38(42) sts.
P 1 row.
Dec row K11(12), k2tog, k12(14), ssk, k11(12).
P 1 row.
Dec row K10(11), k2tog, k12(14), ssk, k10(11).
P 1 row.
Dec row K9(10), k2tog, k12(14), ssk, k9(10).
P 1 row.
Dec row K8(9), k2tog, k12(14), ssk, k8(9). 30(34) sts.
Work 13(17) rows straight.
Shape toes
Cont in M only.
Dec row K1, [k2tog, k5(6)] 4 times, k1.
P 1 row.
Dec row K1, [k2tog, k4(5)] 4 times, k1.
P 1 row.
Dec row K1, [k2tog, k3(4)] 4 times, k1.
P 1 row.
Dec row K1, [k2tog, k2(3)] 4 times, k1.
2nd size only
P 1 row.
Dec row K1, [k2tog, k(2)] 4 times, k1.
Both sizes
Dec row [P2tog] 7 times.
Break yarn, thread through rem sts, pull up and secure. Join seam.

duffel coat

measurements

to fit ages (months)

3–6   6–9   9–12   12–18   18–24

finished measurements

chest

51	56	60	65	70	cm
20	22	23½	25½	27½	in

length to shoulder

24	26	28	32	36	cm
9½	10¼	11	12½	14¼	in

sleeve length

15	17	19	22	24	cm
6	6¾	7½	8¾	9½	in

materials

- 6(7:7:8:8) 50g balls of Debbie Bliss baby cashmerino in Sage Green 019.
- Pair each of 3mm (US 2–3) and 3¼mm (US 3) knitting needles.
- 4 buttons.

tension

26 sts and 44 rows to 10cm/4in square over moss st using 3¼mm (US 3) needles.

abbreviations

y2rn = yarn round needle twice. Also see page 7.

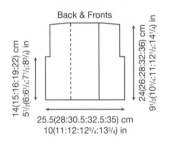

Back & Fronts

14(15:15:16:19:22) cm
5½(6:6¼:7½:8¾) in

25.5(28:30.5:32.5:35) cm
10(11:12:12¾:13¾) in

24(26:28:32:36) cm
9½(10¼:11:12½:14¼) in

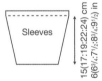

Sleeves

15(17:19:22:24) cm
6(6¾:7½:8¾:9½) in

back

With 3¼mm (US 3) needles, cast on 67(73:79:85:91) sts.
Moss st row K1, [p1, k1] to end.
This row **forms** moss st and is repeated.
Cont in moss st until back measures 14(15:16:19:22)cm/5½(6:6¼:7½:8¾)in from cast on edge, ending with a wrong side row.
Shape armholes
Cast off 4 sts at beg of next 2 rows. 59(65:71:77:83) sts.
Cont straight until back measures 24(26:28:32:36)cm/9½(10¼:11:12½:14¼)in from cast on edge, ending with a wrong side row.
Shape shoulders
Cast off 8(9:10:11:12) sts at beg of next 4 rows.
Cast off rem 27(29:31:33:35) sts.

pocket linings (make 2)

With 3¼mm (US 3) needles, cast on 15(17:17:19:19) sts.
Work 26(28:30:32:34) rows in moss st.
Leave these sts on a holder.

left front

With 3¼mm (US 3) needles, cast on 47(51:55:59:63) sts.
Work 25(27:29:31:33) rows in moss st.

Place pocket

Next row (wrong side) Moss st 28(30:32:34:36), cast off next 15(17:17:19:19) sts, moss st to end.

Next row Moss st 4(4:6:6:8), moss st across 15(17:17:19:19) sts of first pocket lining, moss st 28(30:32:34:36).

Cont in moss st until front measures 14(15:16:19:22)cm/5½(6:6¼:7½:8¾)in from cast on edge, ending with a wrong side row.

Shape armhole

Cast off 4 sts at beg of next row. 43(47:51:55:59) sts.

Cont straight until front measures same as Back to shoulder, ending at armhole edge.

Shape shoulder

Cast off 8(9:10:11:12) sts at beg of next row and foll right side row. Moss st 1 row.

Leave rem 27(29:31:33:35) sts on a spare needle.

Mark position for 4 buttons, the first pair 9(10:11:13:15)cm/3½(4:4¼:5:6)in down from shoulder line, the second pair 6(7:8:9:10)cm/2¼(2¾:3:3½:4)in below the first pair.

right front

Work buttonholes to match markers as follows:

Buttonhole row (right side) Moss st 3, work 2 tog, y2rn, work 2 tog, moss st 14(16:18:20:22), work 2 tog, y2rn, work 2 tog, moss st to end.

With 3¼mm (US 3) needles, cast on 47(51:55:59:63) sts.

Work 25(27:29:31:33) rows in moss st.

Place pocket

Next row (wrong side) Moss st 4(4:6:6:8), cast off next 15(17:17:19:19) sts, moss st to end.

Next row Moss st 28(30:32:34:36), moss st across 15(17:17:19:19) sts of second pocket lining, moss st to end.

Cont in moss st until front measures 14(15:16:19:22)cm/5½(6:6¼:7½:8¾)in from cast on edge, ending with a right side row.

Shape armhole

Cast off 4 sts at beg of next row. 43(47:51:55:59) sts.

Cont straight until front measures same as Back to shoulder, ending at armhole edge.

Shape shoulder

Cast off 8(9:10:11:12) sts at beg of next row and foll wrong side row. 27(29:31:33:35) sts.

Moss st 1 row.

Leave sts on needle for hood.

hood

Join shoulder seams.

Next row (right side) Moss st 27(29:31:33:35) sts from right front, cast on 41(45:47:51:53) sts, moss st 27(29:31:33:35) sts from left front. 95(103:109:117:123) sts.

Cont in moss st until hood measures 18(20:22:24:26)cm/7(8:8¾:9½:10¼)in, ending with a wrong side row. Cast off in moss st.

sleeves

With 3¼mm (US 3) needles, cast on 35(37:41:43:47) sts.

Moss st 14(14:16:16:18) rows.

Place markers at each end of last row.

Change to 3mm (US 2-3) needles.

Moss st 14(14:16:16:18) rows.

Change to 3¼mm (US 3) needles.

Inc and work into moss st, one st at each end of the next row and every foll 6th row until there are 53(57:63:67:73) sts.

Cont straight until sleeve measures 15(17:19:22:24)cm/6(6¾:7½:8¾:9½)in from markers, ending with a wrong side row.

Place markers at each end of last row.

Work a further 8 rows.

Cast off.

to make up

Fold hood in half and join top seam. Easing in fullness, join cast on edge of hood to sts cast off at back neck. Matching centre of cast off edge of sleeve to shoulder, sew sleeves into armholes, with row ends above markers sewn to sts cast off at underarm. Join side and sleeve seams. Sew down pocket linings. Sew on buttons.

blanket

measurements

Approximately 70 x 86cm/27½ x 34in including edging.

materials

- Nine 50g balls of Debbie Bliss baby cashmerino in Ecru 101.
- Pair of 3¼mm (US 3) knitting needles.

tension

25 sts and 34 rows to 10cm/4in square over st st using 3¼mm (US 3) needles.

abbreviations

MB1 = [k1, yf, k1, yf, k1] all into next st, turn, p5, turn, k3, k2tog, pass 3 sts, one at a time, over k2 tog.
MB2 = [k1, p1, k1, p1, k1] all into next st, [turn, sl 1, k4] 4 times, lift 2nd, 3rd, 4th and then 5th st over first st and off needle.
Also see page 7.

tip

If you prefer, use a 3¼mm (US 3) circular needle and work back and forth in rows.

to make

With 3¼mm (US 3) needles, cast on 159 sts.
1st row K to end.
2nd row P to end.
3rd and 4th rows As 1st and 2nd rows.
5th row K2, * yf, skpo, k1, k2tog, yf, k5; rep from * to last 7 sts, yf, skpo, k1, k2tog, yf, k2.
6th row P to end.
7th row K3, * yf, sl 1, k2tog, psso, yf, k7; rep from * to last 6 sts, yf, sl 1, k2tog, psso, yf, k3.
8th row P to end.
9th row K4, * MB1, k9; rep from * to last 5 sts, MB1, k4.
10th row P to end.
11th to 14th rows Rep 1st and 2nd rows twice.
15th row K7, * yf, skpo, k1, k2tog, yf, k5; rep from * to last 2 sts, k2.

16th row P to end.
17th row K8, * yf, sl 1, k2tog, psso, yf, k7; rep from * to last st, k1.
18th row P to end.
19th row K9, * MB1, k9; rep from * to end.
20th row P to end.
These 20 rows **form** the patt and are repeated.
Cont in patt until blanket measures 85cm/33½in from cast on edge, ending with a 4th or 14th row.
Cast off.

edging

With 3¼mm (US 3) needles, cast on 6 sts.
1st row (right side) K3, yf, k3.
2nd and every foll alt row K to end.
3rd row K3, yf, k4.
5th row K3, yf, k5.
7th row K3, yf, k6.
9th row K3, yf, k7.
11th row K3, yf, k7, MB2. 12 sts.
12th row Cast off 6 sts, k to end. 6 sts.
These 6 rows **form** the patt and are repeated.
Cont in patt until edging is long enough to fit around the outer edge of the blanket.
Cast off.

to make up

Sew edging in place. Join cast on edge to cast off edge.

teddy rattle

size

Approximately 6cm/2½in from top to base of head.

materials

- One 50g ball Debbie Bliss baby cashmerino in Camel 021.
- Pair 2¾mm (US 2) knitting needles.
- Washable toy stuffing.
- Black felt and matching sewing thread.
- One large and one small bell.
- 70cm/¾yd narrow ribbon.

tension

29 sts and 60 rows to 10cm/4in square over garter st using 2¾mm (US 2) needles.

abbreviations

See page 7.

tip

If you are not going to hang the rattle out of reach of tiny hands, then do not attach the small bell.

head

Make 1 piece.
With 3mm (US 2-3) needles, cast on 16 sts.
K 1 row.
Next row [Kfb, k2, kfb] 4 times. 24 sts.
K 1 row.
Next row [Kfb, k4, kfb] 4 times. 32 sts.
K 1 row.
Next row [Kfb, k6, kfb] 4 times. 40 sts.
Next row [Kfb, k8, kfb] 4 times. 48 sts.
K 24 rows.
Shape top
Next row [Skpo, k8, k2tog] 4 times. 40 sts.
K 1 row.
Next row [Skpo, k6, k2tog] 4 times. 32 sts.
K 1 row.
Next row [Skpo, k4, k2tog] 4 times. 24 sts.
K 1 row.
Next row [Skpo, k2, k2tog] 4 times. 16 sts.
K 1 row.
Next row [Skpo, k2tog] 4 times. 8 sts.
K 1 row.
Next row [Skpo, k2tog] twice. 4 sts.
Break yarn, thread through rem sts, pull up and secure.

snout

Make 1 piece.
With 2¾mm (US 2) needles, cast on 24 sts. K 6 rows.
Next row [K1, k2tog] to end. 16 sts.
K 1 row.

Next row [K2tog] to end. 8 sts.
K 1 row.
Break yarn, thread through sts, pull up and secure.

ears

Make 2 pieces.
With 3mm (US 2-3) needles, cast on 10 sts. K 4 rows.
Dec 1 st at each end of next row and 2 foll alt rows. 4 sts. K 1 row.
Inc 1 st at each end of next row and 2 foll alt rows. 10 sts. K 3 rows.
Cast off knitwise.

to make up

Gather cast on edge of head and join back seam, leaving a gap. Evenly fill with stuffing placing the larger bell in the centre, close gap in seam. Join snout seam, leaving cast on edge open. Position and sew onto head, stuffing lightly. Fold each ear in half, position on head and sew in place. Cut two small circles from black felt for eyes and one small quarter circle for the nose, then sew in place. Thread the small bell onto the ribbon and tie securely, thread the ribbon through the head, so the bell lies under the chin, then tie the ribbon in a bow.

alphabet cubes

size

Each cube measures 15 x 15 x 15cm/
6 x 6 x 6in.

materials

- One 50g ball of Debbie Bliss
  baby cashmerino in each of
  Pale Blue 202, Teal 203, Pink 600,
  Burnt Orange 023, Pale Green 018
  and Fuchsia 014.
- Pair 3¼ mm (US 3) knitting needles.
- Three 15cm/6in foam cubes.

tension

25 sts and 34 rows to 10cm/4in
square over st st using 3¼ mm
(US 3) needles.

abbreviations

See page 7.

note

Each cube has six faces, three faces
are plain and three have A, B or C.

tip

If you cannot buy 15cm/6in cubes,
use 7.5cm/3in deep foam, cut into
six 15cm/6in blocks and use two
together for each cube.

plain faces (make 3)

** With 3¼ mm (US 3) needles,
cast on 37 sts.
Moss st row K1, [p1, k1] to end.
Rep this row 4 times more.
Next row (wrong side) K1, p1, k1,
p to last 3 sts, k1, p1, k1.
Next row [K1, p1] twice, k to last
4 sts, [p1, k1] twice. **
Rep the last 2 rows 23 times more.
Work 5 rows in moss st across all sts.
Cast off in moss st.

alphabet faces

(Make 3 faces, one in each of A,
B and C)
Work as Plain Face from ** to **.
Rep the last 2 rows 3 times more
then the first of these 2 rows again.
Next row (right side) [K1, p1] twice,
k3, k across 23 sts of 1st row of
chart, k3, [p1, k1] twice.

Next row K1, p1, k1, p4, p across
2nd row of chart, p4, k1, p1, k1.
Working correct chart rows, rep the
last 2 rows until all 31 chart rows
have been worked, so ending with
a right side row.
Next row (wrong side) K1, p1, k1,
p to last 3 sts, k1, p1, k1.
Next row [K1, p1] twice, k to last
4 sts, [p1, k1] twice.
Rep the last 2 rows 3 times more.
Work 5 rows in moss st across all sts.
Cast off in moss st.

to make up

Arrange the knitted faces in the order
you prefer and join the sides of the six
faces as shown. Join the lower five
faces to each other, insert the foam
cube then join the remaining three
sides of the sixth face.

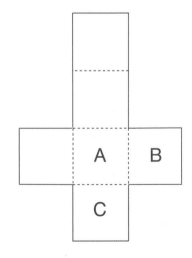

key

☐ Main yarn
▨ Contrast yarn

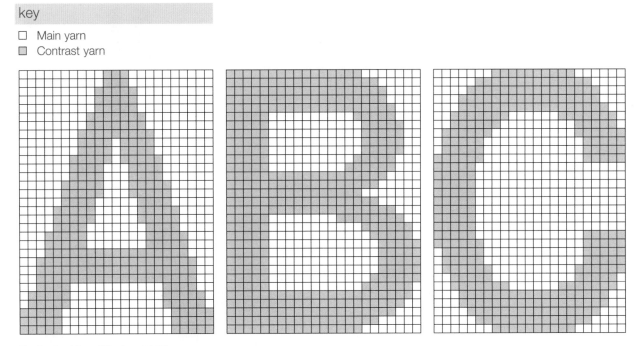

Each chart has 23 sts and 31 rows

bear faced pyjama case

size

Approximately 30cm/12in diameter.

materials

- Three 50g balls of Debbie Bliss baby cashmerino in Camel 21.
- Pair 3¼mm (US 3) knitting needles.
- 40 x 81cm/16 x 32in lining fabric.
- Oddments of black and chocolate brown felt.
- Oddments of chocolate brown yarn for embroidery.
- 3 small Velcro© spots.

tension

25 sts and 44 rows to 10cm/4in square over moss st using 3¼mm (US 3) needles.

abbreviations

kpk = [k1, p1, k1] all into next st. Also see page 7.

bear face front

With 3¼mm (US 3) needles,
cast on 15 sts.
Moss st row K1, [p1, k1] to end.
This row **sets** the moss st.
Next row Kpk, [p1, k1] to last
2 sts, p1, kpk.
Rep the last row 3 times more. 31 sts.
Inc and take into moss st one st at
each end of next 11 rows. 53 sts.
Moss st 1 row.
Inc and take into moss st one st at
each end of next row. 55 sts.
Rep the last 2 rows 7 times more.
69 sts.
Moss st 3 rows.
Inc and take into moss st one st at
each end of next row.
Moss st 3 rows.
Inc and take into moss st one st at
each end of next row.
Moss st 5 rows.
Inc and take into moss st one st at
each end of next row.
Moss st 11 rows.
Inc and take into moss st one st at
each end of next row. 77 sts.
Moss st 17 rows.
** Dec 1 st at each end of next row.
75 sts.
Moss st 11 rows.
Place a marker at each end of
last row.
Dec 1 st at each end of next row.
Moss st 5 rows.
Dec 1 st at each end of next row.
Moss st 3 rows.

Dec 1 st at each end of next row.
Moss st 3 rows.
Dec 1 st at each end of next row.
Moss st 1 row.
Rep the last 2 rows 7 more times.
53 sts.
Dec 1 st at each end of next 11 rows.
Next 4 rows Work 2 tog, work
2tog tbl, moss st to last 4 sts,
work 2tog tbl, work 2 tog. 15 sts.
Cast off in moss st.

bear face back (make 2)

With 3¼mm (US 3) needles,
cast on 77 sts.
Moss st row P1, [k1, p1] to end.
This row **sets** the moss st.
Moss st 18 more rows.
Work exactly as Bear Face from
** to end.
Markers need be placed on only
one back piece.

ears (make 4)

With 3¼mm (US 3) needles,
cast on 9 sts.
Moss st row K1, [p1, k1] to end.
This row **forms** the moss st.
Taking inc sts into moss st, inc 1 st
at each end of next 6 rows. 21 sts.
Moss st 1 row.
Inc 1 st at each end of next row.
Rep the last 2 rows 4 times more.
Moss st 3 rows.

Inc 1 st at each end of next row.
33 sts.
Moss st 6 rows.
Cast off in moss st.

facial features

Cut two 2cm/¾in circles from
brown felt and two 1cm/½in circles
from back felt. Stitch small circles
onto larger circles for eyes, position
on front and stitch in place. Cut a
triangle from brown felt for nose
and stitch in place on front. With
brown yarn, embroider mouth.
See photo for details.

lining

Using the front and backs as
templates, cut lining pieces
adding 1.5cm/⅝in all around.
Folding seam allowances onto
wrong side, slip stitch each
lining piece to its knitted piece.

to make up

Sew ear pieces to front and one back,
using the markers to show the lower
extent of the ear placement. Lay lower
back onto front and join around the
edge. Lay upper back onto front,
overlapping lower back and join
around edge and ears. Stitch across
lower edge of ears, through both
thicknesses. Cut pieces of brown felt
for ear liners and slipstitch in place.

polo shirt

measurements

to fit ages (months)
3–6   6–9   9–12   12–18   18–24

finished measurements

chest
50	55	60	65	70	cm
19¾	21½	23½	25½	27½	in

length to shoulder
24	26	28	32	36	cm
9½	10¼	11	12½	14¼	in

sleeve length
15	17	19	22	24	cm
6	6¾	7½	8¾	9½	in

materials

- 3(3:4:4:4) 50g balls of Debbie Bliss baby cashmerino in Silver 012.
- Pair each of 3mm (US 2-3) and 3¼mm (US 3) knitting needles.
- 3mm (US 2-3) and 3¼mm (US 3) circular needles.
- 2 buttons.

tension

25 sts and 34 rows to 10cm/4in square over st st using 3¼mm (US 3) needles.

abbreviations

See page 7.

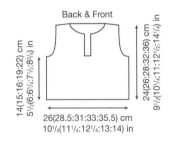

Back & Front

14(15:16:19:22) cm
5½(6:6¼:7½:8¾) in

24(26:28:32:36) cm
9½(10¼:11:12½:14¼) in

26(28.5:31:33:35.5) cm
10¼(11¼:12¼:13:14) in

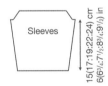

Sleeves

15(17:19:22:24) cm
6(6¾:7½:8¾:9½) in

back

With 3mm (US 2-3) needles, cast on 65(71:77:83:89) sts.
1st rib row K1, [p1, k1] to end.
2nd rib row P1, [k1, p1] to end.
Rep the last 2 rows twice more.

Change to 3¼mm (US 3) needles.
Beg with a k row, work in st st until back measures 14(15:16:19:22)cm/ 5½(6:6¼:7½:8¾)in from cast on edge, ending with a p row.
Shape armholes
Cast off 3(3:3:4:4) sts at beg of next 2 rows. 59(65:71:75:81) sts **.
Next row (right side) K2, skpo, k to last 4 sts, k2tog, k2.
Next row P to end.
Rep the last 2 rows 3(4:5:5:6) times. 51(55:59:63:67) sts.
Cont in st st until back measures 24(26:28:32:36)cm/ 9½(10¼:11:12½:14¼) in from cast on edge, ending with a p row.
Shape shoulders
Cast off 12(13:14:15:16) sts at beg of next 2 rows.
Cast off rem 27(29:31:33:35) sts.

front

Work as given for Back to **.
Divide for front opening
Next row (right side) K2, skpo, k23(26:29:31:34), turn and work on these sts only for first side of front neck, leave rem sts on a spare needle. 26(29:32:34:37) sts.
Next row P to end.
Next row K2, skpo, k to end.
Rep the last 2 rows 2(3:4:4:5) times more. 23(25:27:29:31) sts.
Work straight until front measures 20(22:24:27:31)cm/ 8(8¾:9½:10¾:12¼)in from cast on edge, ending with a k row.

Shape neck

Next row Cast off 7(8:9:10:11) sts, p to end.

Dec one st at neck edge on the next 4 rows. 12(13:14:15:16) sts. Work straight until front measures same as Back to shoulder, ending at armhole edge.

Shape shoulder

Cast off.

With right side facing, rejoin yarn to sts on spare needle, cast off 5 sts at centre front, k to last 4 sts, k2tog, k2.

Next row P to end.

Next row K to last 4 sts, k2tog, k2. Rep the last 2 rows 2(3:4:4:5) times more. 23(25:27:29:31) sts.

Work straight until front measures 20(22:24:27:31)cm/ 8(8¾:9½:10¾:12¼)in from cast on edge, ending with a p row.

Shape neck

Next row Cast off 7(8:9:10:11) sts, k to end.

Dec one st at neck edge on the next 4 rows. 12(13:14:15:16) sts. Work straight until front measures same as Back to shoulder, ending at armhole edge.

Shape shoulder

Cast off.

sleeves

With 3mm (US 2-3) needles, cast on 34(36:38:40:42) sts.

Rib row [K1, p1] to end. Rep the last row 5 times more.

Change to 3¼mm (US 3) needles. Beg with a k row, work in st st. Work 2 rows.

Inc row K3, m1, k to last 3 sts, m1, k3. Work 3 rows.

Rep the last 4 rows 8(10:12:15:18) times more and the inc row again. 54(60:66:74:82) sts.

Cont straight until sleeve measures 15(17:19:22:24)cm/6(6¾:7½:8¾:9½)in from cast on edge, ending with a p row.

Shape sleeve top

Cast off 3(3:3:4:4) sts at beg of next 2 rows. 48(54:60:66:74) sts.

Next row K2, skpo, k to last 4 sts, k2tog, k2.

Next row P to end.

Rep the last 2 rows 3(4:5:5:6) times more. 40(44:48:54:60) sts.

Cast off.

button band

With right side facing and 3mm (US 2–3) needles, pick up and k19(21:23:23:25) sts evenly along right front edge.

1st row K1, [p1, k1] to end.

2nd row P1, [k1, p1] to end.

Rep the last 2 rows 3 times more and the 1st row again.

Cast off in rib.

buttonhole band

With right side facing and 3mm (US 2–3) needles, pick up and 19(21:23:23:25) sts evenly along left front edge.

1st row K1, [p1, k1] to end.

2nd row P1, [k1, p1] to end.

Rep the last 2 rows once more.

Buttonhole row Rib 3, yrn, rib 2tog, rib 8(10:12:12:14), yrn, rib 2 tog, rib 4.

Rib 4 rows.

Cast off in rib.

collar

Join shoulder seams.

With 3mm (US 2–3) circular needle and beg at centre of buttonband, pick up and k23(24:25:26:27) sts up right front to shoulder, 37(39:41:43:45) sts across cast off back neck edge and 23(24:25:26:27) sts down left front to centre of buttonhole band. 83(87:91:95:99) sts.

Next row K1, [p1, k1] to end.

Next 2 rows Rib to last 20 sts, turn.

Next 2 rows Rib to last 15 sts, turn.

Next 2 rows Rib to last 10 sts, turn.

Next 2 rows Rib to last 5 sts, turn.

Change to 3¼mm (US 3) needles. Cont in rib until collar measures 8(8:8:9:9)cm/3(3:3:3½:3½)in from centre back neck.

Cast off in rib.

to make up

Sew sleeves into armholes easing to fit. Join side and sleeve seams. Place lower edge of left front band over lower edge of right front band and sew in place. Sew on buttons.

carryboo

measurements

to fit ages (months)
0–3   3–6

length to top of hood
68   75   cm
26¾   29½   in

materials

- 10(11) 50g balls of Debbie Bliss baby cashmerino in Camel 021.
- Pair each 4½mm (US 7) and 5mm (US 8) knitting needles.
- 1m/1⅛yd of 90cm/36in wide cotton fabric for lining.
- 1m/1⅛yd of satin ribbon.

tension

18 sts and 26 rows to 10cm/4in square over st st using 5mm (US 8) needles and double yarn.

abbreviations

See page 7.

note

The carryboo is worked throughout using two lengths of yarn held together.

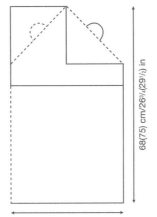

68(75) cm/26¾(29½) in

40(43.5) cm/15¾(17) in

to make

(Worked in one piece)
With 5mm (US 8) needles and double yarn, cast on 145(157) sts.
Moss st row K1, [p1, k1] to end.
This row **forms** moss st and is repeated.
Work a further 5 rows in moss st.
Next row (right side) [K1, p1] twice, k to last 4 sts, [p1, k1] twice.
Next row K1, [p1, k1] twice, p to last 5 sts, [k1, p1] twice, k1.
These 2 rows **form** st st with moss st borders and are repeated.
Cont in patt until work measures 39(43)cm/15¼(17)in, ending with a wrong side row.
Next row (right side) [K1, p1] 38(41) times, k65(71), [p1, k1] twice.
Next row K1, [p1, k1] twice, p63(69), k1, [p1, k1] to end.
Rep the last 2 rows twice more.
Next row (right side) Cast off 72(78) sts in moss st, with 1 st on needle after cast off, moss st 4, k to last 4 sts, [p1, k1] twice. 73(79) sts.
Next row (wrong side) K1, [p1, k1] twice, p to last 5 sts, [k1, p1] twice, k1.
Next row [K1, p1] twice, k to last 4 sts, [p1, k1] twice.
Rep the last 2 rows until work measures 66(73)cm/26(28¾)in from cast on edge, ending with a wrong side row.
Work 5 rows in moss st across all sts.
Cast off in moss st.

ears (make 2)

With 4½mm (US 7) needles and double yarn, cast on 17 sts.
Moss st row K1, [p1, k1] to end.
Rep this row once more.
Next row K1, p1, k to last 2 sts, p1, k1.
Next row K1, p1, k1, p to last 3 sts, k1, p1, k1.
Rep the last 2 rows once more.
Next row K1, p1, ssk, k to last 4 sts, k2tog, p1, k1.
Next row K1, p1, k1, p to last 3 sts, k1, p1, k1.
Rep the last 2 rows 4 times more. 7 sts.
Next row K1, p1, sl 1, k2tog, psso, p1, k1.
5 sts.
Moss st 1 row.
Next row K1, p1, kpk, p1, k1. 7 sts.
Moss st 1 row.
Next row K1, p1, kfb, kfb, k1, p1, k1. 9 sts.
Next row K1, p1, k1, p to last 3 sts, k1, p1, k1.
Next row K1, p1, kfb, k to last 4 sts, kfb, k1, p1, k1.
Rep the last 2 rows 3 times more. 17 sts.
Next row K1, p1, k1, p to last 3 sts, k1, p1, k1.
Next row K1, p1, k to last 2 sts, p1, k1.
Rep the last 2 rows once more.
Moss st 1 row.
Cast off in moss st.

Fold ears in half across the centre and stitch around the edges.

lining

Using the knitted piece as a template, cut a piece of lining fabric the same shape adding 1.5cm/⅝in all around. Neaten all fabric edges by pressing under the 1.5cm/⅝in seam allowance and slipstitch in place to knitted piece around all edges.

to make up

Place markers on side edges, 30cm/12in up from cast on edge. Fold in half along cast on edge and stitch to form lower edge of bag then continue seam up the side edges to markers, leaving edges above markers open. Cut ribbon in half and sew one piece to the corner of the front edge and the remaining piece to the back. Fold cast off top edge in half and join seam to form top of hood. Lay carryboo flat, so the hood forms a triangle. Measure 10cm/4in down from the tip of the hood along the folded edges and place a marker, then stitch the ears in place with the top of the ear at the marker.

cable tank top

measurements

to fit ages (months)
3–6   6–9   9–12   12–18   18–24

finished measurements

chest

43	50	55	62	67	cm
17	19¾	21¾	24½	26½	in

length to shoulder

22	24	26	28	30	cm
8¾	9½	10¼	11	11¾	in

materials

- 2(3:3:3:4) 50g balls of Debbie Bliss baby cashmerino in Pale Blue 202 (M) and one 50g ball in Ecru 101 (C).
- Pair each 3mm (US 2-3) and 3¼mm (US 3) knitting needles.
- Cable needle.

tensions

25 sts and 34 rows over st st and 32 sts and 34 rows over patt, both to 10cm/4in square using 3¼mm (US 3) needles.

abbreviations

C4F = slip next 2 sts onto cable needle and hold to front of work, k2, then k2 from cable needle.
m1p = make 1 st by picking up and purling into back of loop lying between st just worked and next st. Also see page 7.

Back & Front

12(13:14:17:19) cm
4¾(5:5½:6¾:7½) in

22(24:26:28:30) cm
8¾(9½:10¼:11:11¾) in

22(25.5:28:32:34.5) cm
8¾(10:11:12½:13½) in

back

With 3mm (US 2-3) needles and C, cast on 58(66:74:82:90) sts.
1st row K2, [p2, k2] to end.
2nd row P2, [k2, p2] to end.
These 2 rows **form** the rib.
Change to M.
Rib a further 4 rows.
Change to C.
Rib a further 2 rows.
Cont in M.
Rib 1 row.

Inc row (wrong side) P2, k2(0:2:0:2), p2(0:2:0:2), * k2, m1p, p2, m1p, k2, p2; rep from * to last 4(0:4:0:4) sts, k2(0:2:0:2), p2(0:2:0:2).
70(82:90:102:110) sts.
Change to 3¼mm (US 3) needles.
Cont in patt as follows:
1st row K2, p2(0:2:0:2), k2(0:2:0:2), * p2, k4, p2, k2; rep from * to last 4(0:4:0:4) sts, p2(0:2:0:2), k2(0:2:0:2).
2nd row P2, k2(0:2:0:2), p2(0:2:0:2), * k2, p4, k2, p2; rep from * to last 4(0:4:0:4) sts, k2(0:2:0:2), p2(0:2:0:2).
3rd row K2, p2(0:2:0:2), k2(0:2:0:2), * p2, C4F, p2, k2; rep from * to last 4(0:4:0:4) sts, p2(0:2:0:2), k2(0:2:0:2).
4th row As 2nd row.
5th row As 1st row.
6th row As 2nd row.
These 6 rows **form** the patt and are repeated.
All sizes
Cont in patt until back measures 12(13:14:17:19)cm/4¾(5:5½:6¾:7½)in from cast on edge, ending with a wrong side row.
Shape armholes
Cast off 3 sts at beg of next 2 rows. 64(76:84:96:104) sts. **
Dec one st at each end of the next row and 3(5:5:9:9) foll right side rows. 56(64:72:76:84) sts.
Cont in patt until back measures 22(24:26:28:30)cm/ 8¾(9½:10¼:11:11¾)in from cast on edge, ending with a wrong side row.

Shape shoulders

Cast off 8(9:10:10:11) sts at beg of next 2 rows and 9(10:11:11:12) sts at beg of foll 2 rows.
Leave rem 22(26:30:34:38) sts on a holder.

front

Work as given for Back to **.

Shape front neck

Next row Work 2 tog, patt 27(33:37:43:47) sts, k2tog, turn and work on these 29(35:39:45:49) sts only for first side of neck, leave rem sts on a spare needle.
Next row Patt to end.
Next row Work 2 tog, patt to last 2 sts, k2tog.
Rep the last 2 rows 2(4:4:8:8) times more. 23(25:29:27:31) sts.
Keeping armhole edge straight, dec one st at neck edge on every foll right side row until 17(19:21:21:23) sts rem.
Cont straight until front measures same as Back to shoulder, ending at armhole edge.

Shape shoulder

Cast off 8(9:10:10:11) sts at beg of next row.
Work 1 row.
Cast off rem 9(10:11:11:12) sts.
With right side facing, slip centre 2 sts onto a safety pin, rejoin yarn to rem 31(37:41:47:51) sts on spare needle, skpo, patt to last 2 sts, work 2 tog.
Next row Patt to end.
Next row Skpo, patt to last 2 sts, work 2 tog.

Rep the last 2 rows 2(4:4:8:8) times more. 23(25:29:27:31) sts.
Keeping armhole edge straight, dec one st at neck edge on every foll right side row until 17(19:21:21:23) sts rem.
Cont straight until front measures same as Back to shoulder, ending at armhole edge.

Shape shoulder

Cast off 8(9:10:10:11) sts at beg of next row.
Work 1 row.
Cast off rem 9(10:11:11:12) sts.

neckband

Join right shoulder seam.
With right side facing, 3mm (US 2-3) needles and M, pick up and k36(38:40:44:46) sts evenly down left front neck, k2 from safety pin, pick up and k34(36:38:42:44) sts evenly up right side of front neck, then across 22(26:30:34:38) sts on back neck holder, work: p0(0:0:0:2), [k2tog] 0(0:0:2:2) times, k0(0:2:0:0), p0(2:2:2:2), k2, p2, [k2 tog] twice, p2, k2, p2, [k2 tog] twice, p2, k2, p0(2:2:2:2), k0(0:2:0:0), [k2tog] 0(0:0:2:2) times, p0(0:0:0:2). 90(98:106:114:122) sts.
Change to C.

1st, 3rd and 4th sizes only
1st row P2, [k2, p2] to end.
2nd and 5th sizes only
1st row K2, [p2, k2] to end.
All sizes
This row **sets** the rib patt.

2nd row Rib 35(37:39:43:45), k2tog, skpo, rib to end.
Change to M.
3rd row Rib to end.
4th row Rib 34(36:38:42:44), k2tog, skpo, rib to end.
Change to C.
5th row Rib to end.
6th row Rib 33(35:37:41:43), k2tog, skpo, rib to end.
7th row Rib to end.
8th row Rib 32(34:36:40:42), k2tog, skpo, rib to end.
Change to M.
9th row Rib to end.
10th row Cast off in rib, decreasing on this row as before.

armbands

Join right shoulder seam and neckband seam.
With right side facing, 3mm (US 2-3) needles and M, pick up and k78(82:86:94:98) sts evenly around armhole edge.
Change to C.
1st row K2, [p2, k2] to end.
2nd row P2, [k2, p2] to end.
These 2 rows **form** the rib patt and are repeated.
Work 2 rows M, 4 rows C, and 1 row M.
With M, cast off in rib.

to make up

Join side and armband seams.

lucy locket dress

measurements

to fit ages (months)
6–12   12–18   18–24

finished measurements

chest

51	57	60	cm
20	22½	23½	in

length to shoulder

39	45	50	cm
15¼	17¾	19¾	in

sleeve length

4	4	5	cm
1½	1½	2	in

materials

- 6(7:8) 50g balls Debbie Bliss baby cashmerino in Peach 022.
- Pair each 2¾mm (US 2), 3mm (US 2–3) and 3¼mm (US 3) knitting needles.
- 2¾mm (US 2) circular needle.
- 1 button.
- 35cm/14in of narrow ribbon.

tension

26 sts and 44 rows using 3¼mm (US 3) needles and 27 sts and 46 rows using 3mm (US 2–3) both to 10cm/4in square over moss st.

abbreviations

See page 7.

26.5(29.5:30.5) cm
10½(11½:12) in

28(33:37) cm
11(13:14½) in

39(45:50) cm
15¼(17¾:19¾) in

Back & Front

Sleeves

4(4:5) cm
1½(1½:2) in

back

With 3¼mm (US 3) needles,
cast on 105(117:123) sts.

Moss st row (right side) K1, [p1, k1]
to end.

This row **forms** the moss st.

Cont straight until back measures
23(27:31)cm/9(10¾:12¼)in from
cast on edge, ending with
a wrong side row.

Dec row K1, p1, k1, [p3tog, k1, p1,
k1] 17(19:20) times. 71(79:83) sts.

Change to 3mm (US 2-3) needles.

Cont straight in moss st until back
measures 28(33:37)cm/11(13:14½)in
from cast on edge, ending with
a wrong side row.

Shape armholes

Cast off 5(6:6) sts at beg of next
2 rows. 61(67:71) sts.

Dec one st at each end of the
next row and every foll right side row
until 49(53:57) sts rem.

Moss st 7 rows.

Back opening

Next row (right side) Moss st
23(25:27) sts, turn and work on these
sts only for first side of back opening,
leave rem 26(28:30) sts on a spare
needle or holder.

Next row Cast on 3 sts, moss st
these 3 sts, then moss st to end.
26(28:30) sts.

Cont in moss st until back measures
36(42:47)cm/14¼(16½:18½)in from
cast on edge ending with a wrong
side row.

Shape neck

Next row Moss st to last 8(9:10) sts,
leave these sts on a holder, turn and
cont on rem 18(19:20) sts.

Dec one st at neck edge on next
4 rows. 14(15:16) sts.

Cont straight until back measures
38(44:49)cm/15(17¼:19¼)in from
cast on edge, ending with a wrong
side row.

Shape shoulder

Cast off.

With right side facing, rejoin yarn to
rem 26(28:30) sts, moss st to end.

Cont in moss st until back measures
36(42:47)cm/14¼(16½:18½)in from
cast on edge ending with a wrong
side row.

Shape neck

Next row Moss st 8(9:10) sts, leave
these sts on a holder, moss st to end.

Dec one st at neck edge on next
4 rows. 14(15:16) sts.

Cont straight until back measures
38(44:49)cm/15(17¼:19¼)in from
cast on edge, ending with
a wrong side row.

Shape shoulder

Cast off.

front

Work as given for Back until front
measures 30(36:41)cm/11¾(14¼:16)in
from cast on edge, ending with a
wrong side row.

Shape neck

Next row Moss st 18(19:20) sts,
turn and work on these sts only for
first side of neck shaping, leave rem
31(34:37) sts on a spare needle.

Dec one st at neck edge on 4 foll
right side rows. 14(15:16) sts.

Cont without further shaping until front
measures same as Back to shoulder,
ending at side edge.

Shape shoulder

Cast off.

With right side facing, slip centre
13(15:17) sts onto a holder, rejoin
yarn to rem 18(19:20) sts on spare
needle, moss st to end.

Complete to match first side,
reversing shapings.

sleeves

With 3¼mm (US 3) needles,
cast on 65(71:77) sts.
Moss st row K1, [p1, k1] to end.
Rep this row 13(13:15) times more.
Shape top
Cast off 5(6:6) sts at beg of next
2 rows. 55(59:65) sts.
Cast off 2 sts at beg of next
24(26:28) rows.
Cast off rem 7(7:9) sts

pocket

With 3¼mm (US 3) needles,
cast on 23 sts.
Moss st row K1, [p1, k1] to end.
Next row K1, m1, moss st to last st,
m1, k1.
Next row Moss st to end.
Rep the last 2 rows 5 times more.
35 sts.
Work a further 27 rows moss st.
Change to 3mm (US 2-3) needles.
Next row K3, [k2tog, k2] 8 times.
27 sts.
K 3 rows.
Cast off row Cast off 4 sts, * slip st
back onto left hand needle, cast on
2 sts, cast off 5 sts; rep from * to end.

neckband

Join shoulder seams.
With right side facing and 2¾mm
(US 2) circular needle, slip 8(9:10) sts
from left back onto needle, pick up
and k7 sts up left back to shoulder,
17 sts down left front neck, k across
13(15:17) sts from front neck holder,
pick up and k17 sts up right front
neck to shoulder, 7 sts from right
back neck, k across 8(9:10) sts on
back neck holder. 77(81:85) sts.
Work backwards and forwards in rows.
K 1 row.
Buttonhole row K1, k2tog, yf,
k to end.
K 1 row.
Cast off.

sleeve edgings

With right side facing and 2¾mm
(US 2) needles, pick up and
k40(43:46) sts along cast on edge.
K 3 rows.
Cast off row Cast off 4 sts, * slip st
back onto left hand needle, cast on
2 sts, cast off 5 sts; rep from * to end.

lower edgings

With right side facing and 2¾mm
(US 2) circular needle, pick up and
k105(117:123) sts along cast on edge.
K 3 rows.

Cast off row Cast off 4 sts, * slip st
back onto left hand needle, cast on
2 sts, cast off 5 sts; rep from * to end.

to make up

Sew sleeves into armholes. Join side
and sleeve seams. Lap button band
behind buttonhole band and catch in
place at lower edge. Sew on button.
Run a line of gathering stitches around
pocket edge and slipstitch in place.
Cut ribbon in half and thread through
garter stitch top edge to tie at centre.

star and heart sweaters

measurements

to fit ages (months)

3–6	6–9	9–12	12–18	18–24

finished measurements

chest

50	55	60	65	70	cm
19¾	21¾	23½	25½	27½	in

length to shoulder

25	27	29	33	37	cm
9¾	10¾	11½	13	14½	in

sleeve length

15	17	19	22	24	cm
6	6¾	7½	8¾	9 ½	in

materials

- 3(3:3:4:4) 50g balls of Debbie Bliss baby cashmerino in Pale Blue 202 **or** Pale Pink 600.
- Pair each of 3mm (US 2–3) and 3¼mm (US 3) knitting needles.
- 4 small buttons.

tension

25 sts and 34 rows to 10cm/4in square over st st using 3¼mm (US 3) needles.

abbreviations

See page 7.

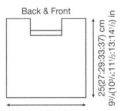

Back & Front

25(27:29:33:37) cm
9¾(10¾:11½:13:14½) in

26(28.5:31:33:35.5) cm
10¼(11¼:12¼:13:14) in

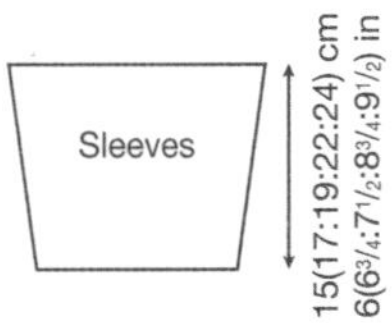

Sleeves

15(17:19:22:24) cm
6(6¾:7½:8¾:9½) in

front

With 3mm (US 2-3) needles, cast on 65(71:77:83:89) sts.
K 7 rows.
Change to 3¼mm (US 3) needles.
Next row (right side) K to end.
Next row K4, p to last 4 sts, k4.
Rep the last 2 rows 4 times more.
Beg with a k row, work in st st until front measures 6(7:8:10:12)cm/ 2¼(2¾:3:4:4¾)in from cast on edge, ending with a p row.

Place motif chart
1st row (right side) K21(24:27:30:33), work across 1st row of chart, k21(24:27:30:33).
2nd row P21(24:27:30:33), work across 2nd row of chart, p21(24:27:30:33).
These 2 rows **set** the position of the chart.
Work a further 27 rows.
Next row (wrong side) P5, k4, p12(15:18:21:24), work across 30th row of chart, p12(15:18:21:24), k4, p5.
Next row K21(24:27:30:33), work across 31st row of chart, k21(24:27:30:33).
Work in patt as set by the last 2 rows to the end of chart.
Next row (right side) K to end.
Next row P5, k4, p to last 9 sts, k4, p5. **
Rep the last 2 rows until front measures 20(22:24:27:31)cm/ 8(8¾:9½:10¾:12¼)in from cast on edge, ending with a k row.
Next row P5, k4, p7(9:11:13:15), k33(35:37:39:41), p7(9:11:13:15), k4, p5.
Next row K to end.
Rep the last 2 rows once more.

Shape neck
Next row (wrong side) P5, k4, p7(9:11:13:15), k4, cast off 25(27:29:31:33) knitwise, with one st on needle after cast off, k next 3 sts, p7(9:11:13:15), k4, p5.
Work on the last set of 20(22:24:26:28) sts for left side of neck.
Next row K20(22:24:26:28).
Next row K4, p7(9:11:13:15), k4, p5.
Next row K to end.
Rep the last 2 rows 5(5:5:6:6) times more.

Buttonhole band
K 1 row.
Next row K6(7:8:9:10), yf, k2tog, k8(9:10:11:12), yf, k2tog, k2.
K 2 rows.
Cast off.
With right side facing, rejoin yarn to rem 20(22:24:26:28) sts, k to end.
Next row P5, k4, p7(9:11:13:15), k4.
Next row K to end.
Rep the last 2 rows 5(5:5:6:6) times more.

Buttonhole band
K 1 row.
Next row K2, k2tog, yf, k8(9:10:11:12), k2tog, yf, k6(7:8:9:10).
K 2 rows. Cast off.

back

Work as given for Front to **, omitting motif.
Rep the last 2 rows until back measures 22(24:26:29:33)cm/ 8¾(9½:10¼:11½:13)in from cast on edge, ending with a k row.
Next row P5, k4, p7(9:11:13:15), k33(35:37:39:41), p7(9:11:13:15), k4, p5.
Next row K to end.
Rep the last 2 rows once more.

Shape neck
Next row (wrong side) P5, k4, p7(9:11:13:15), k4, cast off 25(27:29:31:33) knitwise, with one st on needle after cast off, k next 3 sts, p7(9:11:13:15), k4, p5.
Work on the last set of 20(22:24:26:28) sts for right side of neck.
Next row K20(22:24:26:28).
Next row K4, p7(9:11:13:15), k4, p5.
Next row K to end.
Rep the last 2 rows 2(2:2:3:3) times more.

Buttonband
K 4 rows.
Cast off.
With right side facing, rejoin yarn to rem 20(22:24:26:28) sts, k to end.
Next row P5, k4, p7(9:11:13:15), k4.
Next row K to end.
Rep the last 2 rows 2(2:2:3:3) times more.

Buttonband
K 4 rows.
Cast off.

sleeves

With 3mm (US 2-3) needles,
cast on 34(36:38:40:42) sts.
K 7 rows.
Change to 3¼mm (US 3) needles.
Beg with a k row, work in st st.
Work 2 rows.
Inc row K3, m1, k to last 3 sts,
m1, k3.
Work 3 rows.
Rep the last 4 rows 8(10:12:14:16)
times more and the inc row again.
54(60:66:72:78) sts.
Cont straight until sleeve measures
15(17:19:22:24)cm/6(6¾:7½:8¾:9½)in
from cast on edge, ending with
a p row.
Cast off.

to make up

Lap buttonhole bands over button
bands and catch together at outside
edge. With centre of cast off edge of
sleeve to shoulder, sew on sleeves.
Join sleeve seams. Join side seams
to top of garter st opening.
Sew on buttons.

key

☐ K on right side and P on wrong side rows
▦ P on right side and K on wrong side rows

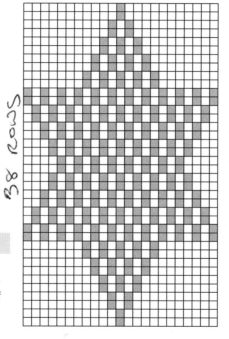
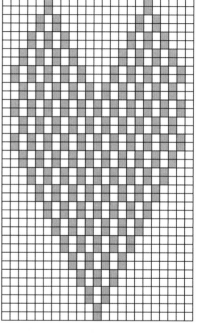

distributors

For stockists of Debbie Bliss
yarns please contact:

UK & Worldwide Distributors

Designer Yarns Ltd
Units 8-10
Newbridge Industrial Estate
Pitt Street, Keighley
W. Yorkshire BD21 4PQ
UK
Tel: +44 (0)1535 664222
Fax: +44 (0)1535 664333
www.designeryarns.uk.com
enquiries@designeryarns.uk.com

USA

Knitting Fever Inc.
315 Bayview Avenue
Amityville
NY 11701
USA
Tel: +1 516 546 3600
Fax +1 516 546 6871
www.knittingfever.com

Hong Kong

East Unity Company Ltd
Unit B2
7/F Block B
Kailey Industrial Centre
12 Fung Yip Street
Chan Wan
Hong Kong
Tel: (852) 2869 7110
Fax: (852) 2537 6952
eastunity@yahoo.com.hk

Germany/Austria/ Switzerland/Benelux

Designer Yarns (Deutschland) GmbH
Welserstrasse 10g
D-51149 Köln
Germany
Tel: +49 (0) 2203 1021910
Fax: +49 (0) 2203 1023551
www.designeryarns.de
info@designeryarns.de

Brazil

Quatro Estacoes Com
Las Linhas e Acessorios Ltda
Av. Das Nacoes Unidas
12551-9 Andar
Cep 04578-000 Sao Paulo
Brazil
Tel: +55 11 3443 7736
cristina@4estacoeslas.com.br

Mexico

Estambres Crochet SA de CV
Aaron Saenz 1891-7
Col. Santa Maria
Monterrey
N.L. 64650
Mexico
Tel: +52 81 8335 3870
abremer@redmundial.com.mx

Sweden

Nysta garn och textil
Hogasvagen 20
S-131 47 Nacka
Sweden
Tel: +46 708 81 39 54
www.nysta.se
info@nysta.se

Canada

Diamond Yarn Ltd
155 Martin Ross Avenue
Unit 3
Toronto
Ontario M3J 2L9
Canada
Tel: +1 416 736 6111
Fax: +1 416 736 6112
www.diamondyarn.com

Russia

Golden Fleece Ltd
Soloviyny proezd 16
117593 Moscow
Russian Federation
Tel: +8 (903) 000-1967
www.rukodelie.ru
natalya@rukodelie.ru

France

Plassard Diffusion
La Filature
71800 Varennes-sous-Dun
France
Tel: +33 (0) 3 85282828
Fax: +33 (0) 3 85282829
info@laines-plassard.com

Finland

Eiran Tukku
Mäkelänkatu 54 B
00510 Helsinki
Finland
Tel: +358 50 346 0575
maria.hellbom@eirantukku.fi

Spain

Oyambre Needlework SL
Balmes, 200 At.4
08006 Barcelona
Spain
Tel: +34 (0) 93 487 26 72
Fax: +34 (0) 93 218 6694
info@oyambreonline.com

Denmark

Fancy Knit
Hovedvejen 71
8586 Oerum Djurs
Ramten
Denmark
Tel: +45 59 4621 89
roenneburg@mail.dk

Norway

Viking of Norway
Bygdaveien 63
4333 Oltedal
Tel: +47 516 11 660
Fax: +47 516 16 235
post@viking-garn.no
www.viking-garn.no

Iceland

Storkurinn ehf
Laugavegi 59
101 Reykjavík
Iceland
Tel: +354 551 8258
Fax: +354 562 8252
storkurinn@simnet.is

Australia/New Zealand

Prestige Yarns Pty Ltd
P O Box 39
Bulli NSW 2516
Australia
Tel: +61 02 4285 6669
www.prestigeyarns.com
info@prestigeyarns.com

Taiwan

U-Knit
1F
199-1 Sec
Zhong Xiao East Road
Taipei
Taiwan
Tel: + 886 2 27527557
Fax: +886 2 27528556
shuindigo@hotmail.com

Thailand

Needle World Co Ltd
Pradit Manoontham Road
Bangkok 10310
Thailand
Tel: 662 933 9167
Fax: 662 933 9110
needle-world.coltd@googlemail.com

China

Lotus Textile Co Ltd
77 Zhonghua W. St.
Xingtai
Hebei
China
05-4000
hanpsheng@yahoo.com.cn

For more information on my other
books and yarns, please visit:
www.debbieblissonline.com